Pursuit of Proverbs

PRESENTED BY
THE PROVERBS 31:26 MINISTRY

Written by:

ANGIE TAYLOR REAMES

Presented to

_____

From

_____

Date: _____

This book is dedicated to those who need encouragement on getting through their next 31days. Regardless of what it is that you are in need of or you feel that you are lacking in this season. It is my prayer that you gain clarity, confirmation, and the inspiration that you need during this time. You are blessed, be encouraged.

This Pursuit of Proverbs is to enhance your prayer life one day at a time. This guide highlights PROVERBS for the next 31 days. What does that mean? Proverbs has 31 chapters. For the next 31 days, you will receive a scripture from each chapter. You will have an opportunity to apply scriptures to your life daily, along with gaining wisdom. Prayer is necessary and purposeful. Never stop where you are- there is so much greatness prepared for where you are going. Keep praying, keep believing, keep trusting.

Biblical content is from the New International Version of the Bible.

The Proverbs 31:26 Ministry, LLC is a ministry founded by Angie Taylor Reames. It is branded by the scripture which promotes wisdom and kindness as this Woman of God has vowed to "Speak with Wisdom" and encourages with "Faithful Instruction on Her Tongue". The Proverbs 31:26 Ministry, LLC was founded in hopes to encourage others to speak positively different, show kindness, use wisdom, show respect, and be the best version of yourself. It is branded to provide clarity, love, and God. Angie encourages women through her transparency and testimony. She embraces with love and confidence in knowing that "God is so intentional", her tag line of ministry.

The ministry supports and leads community involvement. It is a breeding ground for those that are searching for love, confidence, empathy, prayer, and most of all God.

Day 1

PROVERBS 1

Proverbs 1:7 The fear of the Lord is the beginning of knowledge, but fools[a] despise wisdom and instruction.

Today I am thankful for:

_____

_____

_____

_____

_____

_____

_____

_____

_____

_____

People to pray for/ Prayer requests:

_____

_____

_____

_____

_____

_____

_____

_____

_____

_____

Challenges that I may face today:

_____

_____

_____

_____

_____

_____

_____

_____

_____

_____

Reflections about my day:

_____

_____

_____

_____

_____

_____

_____

_____

_____

> **YOU MAY NOT ALWAYS GET IT RIGHT, BUT DON'T GET STUCK BEING WRONG**
>
> Elder Angie Taylor Reames

Day 2

PROVERBS 2

Proverbs 2:12 Wisdom will save you from the ways of wicked men, from men whose words are perverse.

Today I am thankful for:

_____
_____
_____
_____
_____
_____
_____
_____
_____
_____

People to pray for/ Prayer requests:

_____
_____
_____
_____
_____
_____
_____
_____
_____
_____

Challenges that I may face today:

_____

_____

_____

_____

_____

_____

_____

_____

_____

_____

Reflections about my day:

_____

_____

_____

_____

_____

_____

_____

_____

_____

_____

> ## TODAY WILL BE A BLESSED DAY, WALK WITH GOD
>
> Elder Angie Taylor Reames

Day 3

PROVERBS 3

Proverbs 3:5-6 Trust in the LORD with all your heart and lean not on your own understanding; in all your ways submit to him, and he will make your paths straight.

Today I am thankful for:

_____

_____

_____

_____

_____

_____

_____

_____

_____

People to pray for/ Prayer requests:

_____

_____

_____

_____

_____

_____

_____

_____

_____

Challenges that I may face today:

_____
_____
_____
_____
_____
_____
_____
_____
_____
_____

Reflections about my day:

_____
_____
_____
_____
_____
_____
_____
_____
_____
_____

> **YOU ARE LOVED, YOU ARE GOOD ENOUGH, AND YOU MATTER**
>
> Elder Angie Taylor Reames

Day 4

PROVERBS 4

Proverbs 4:26 Give careful thought to the[a] paths for your feet and be steadfast in all your ways.

Today I am thankful for:

_____

_____

_____

_____

_____

_____

_____

_____

_____

People to pray for/ Prayer requests:

_____

_____

_____

_____

_____

_____

_____

_____

_____

Challenges that I may face today:

_____

_____

_____

_____

_____

_____

_____

_____

_____

_____

Reflections about my day:

_____

_____

_____

_____

_____

_____

_____

_____

_____

> **I LOVE YOU, TODAY SHARE THOSE WORDS WITH OTHERS, IT IS NECESSARY**
>
> Elder Angie Taylor Reames

Day 5

PROVERBS 5

Proverbs 5:11 At the end of your life you will groan, when your flesh and body are spent.

Today I am thankful for:

_____

_____

_____

_____

_____

_____

_____

_____

_____

People to pray for/ Prayer requests:

_____

_____

_____

_____

_____

_____

_____

_____

_____

Challenges that I may face today:

_____
_____
_____
_____
_____
_____
_____
_____
_____
_____

Reflections about my day:

_____
_____
_____
_____
_____
_____
_____
_____
_____
_____

> **YOU ARE SO IMPORTANT, STOP BEATING YOURSELF UP WHEN GOD HAS FORGIVEN YOU**
>
> Elder Angie Taylor Reames

"

Day 6

PROVERBS 6

Proverbs 6:16-19 here are six things the LORD hates, seven that are detestable to him: haughty eyes, a lying tongue, hands that shed innocent blood, a heart that devises wicked schemes, feet that are quick to rush into evil, a false witness who pours out lies and a person who stirs up conflict in the community.

Today I am thankful for:

_____

_____

_____

_____

_____

_____

_____

_____

People to pray for/ Prayer requests:

_____

_____

_____

_____

_____

_____

_____

_____

Challenges that I may face today:

_____
_____
_____
_____
_____
_____
_____
_____
_____
_____
_____

Reflections about my day:

_____
_____
_____
_____
_____
_____
_____
_____
_____
_____

> **PAY IT FORWARD TODAY, SOMEONE IS DEPENDING ON YOU TO GET THEM PASS THE PAIN. SHARE YOUR TESTIMONY**
>
> Elder Angie Taylor Reames

Day 7

PROVERBS 7

Proverbs 7:2 Keep my commands and you will live; guard my teachings as the apple of your eye.

Today I am thankful for:

_____

_____

_____

_____

_____

_____

_____

_____

_____

_____

People to pray for/ Prayer requests:

_____

_____

_____

_____

_____

_____

_____

_____

_____

_____

Challenges that I may face today:

_____

_____

_____

_____

_____

_____

_____

_____

_____

_____

_____

Reflections about my day:

_____

_____

_____

_____

_____

_____

_____

_____

_____

_____

> **YOU ARE NOT YOUR LAST MISTAKE, FORGIVE YOURSELF, SO YOU CAN HEAL**
>
> Elder Angie Taylor Reames

Day 8

PROVERBS 8

Proverbs 8:13 To fear the LORD is to hate evil; I hate pride and arrogance, evil behavior and perverse speech.

Today I am thankful for:

_____
_____
_____
_____
_____
_____
_____
_____
_____

People to pray for/ Prayer requests:

_____
_____
_____
_____
_____
_____
_____
_____
_____

Challenges that I may face today:

_____

_____

_____

_____

_____

_____

_____

_____

_____

_____

Reflections about my day:

_____

_____

_____

_____

_____

_____

_____

_____

_____

> **SHARE A SMILE TODAY AND GIVE A FEW LAUGHS, BE INTENTIONAL**
>
> Elder Angie Taylor Reames

Day 9

PROVERBS 9

Proverbs 9:10 The fear of the LORD is the beginning of wisdom, and knowledge of the Holy One is understanding.

Today I am thankful for:

_____

_____

_____

_____

_____

_____

_____

_____

_____

People to pray for/ Prayer requests:

_____

_____

_____

_____

_____

_____

_____

_____

_____

Challenges that I may face today:

_____
_____
_____
_____
_____
_____
_____
_____
_____
_____

Reflections about my day:

_____
_____
_____
_____
_____
_____
_____
_____
_____
_____

GOD IS SO INTENTIONAL

Elder Angie Taylor Reames

Day 10

PROVERBS 10

Proverbs 10:27 The fear of the LORD adds length to life, but the years of the wicked are cut short.

Today I am thankful for:

_____

_____

_____

_____

_____

_____

_____

_____

_____

_____

People to pray for/ Prayer requests:

_____

_____

_____

_____

_____

_____

_____

_____

_____

_____

Challenges that I may face today:

_____
_____
_____
_____
_____
_____
_____
_____
_____
_____
_____

Reflections about my day:

_____
_____
_____
_____
_____
_____
_____
_____
_____
_____

YOU MATTER TOO

Elder Angie Taylor Reames

Day 11

PROVERBS 11

Proverbs 11:25 A generous person will prosper; whoever refreshes others will be refreshed.

Today I am thankful for:

_____

_____

_____

_____

_____

_____

_____

_____

_____

People to pray for/ Prayer requests:

_____

_____

_____

_____

_____

_____

_____

_____

_____

_____

Challenges that I may face today:

_____

_____

_____

_____

_____

_____

_____

_____

_____

_____

Reflections about my day:

_____

_____

_____

_____

_____

_____

_____

_____

_____

> **TRUST GOD EVEN WHEN YOU DON'T UNDERSTAND HIS PLAN**
>
> Elder Angie Taylor Reames

Day 12

PROVERBS 12

Proverbs 12:25 Anxiety weighs down the heart, but a kind word cheers it up.

Today I am thankful for:

_____
_____
_____
_____
_____
_____
_____
_____
_____

People to pray for/ Prayer requests:

_____
_____
_____
_____
_____
_____
_____
_____
_____

Challenges that I may face today:

_____
_____
_____
_____
_____
_____
_____
_____
_____
_____
_____

Reflections about my day:

_____
_____
_____
_____
_____
_____
_____
_____
_____
_____

> **DO SOMETHING FOR YOURSELF TODAY, YOU MATTER TOO**
>
> Elder Angie Taylor Reames

Day 13

PROVERBS 13

Proverbs 13:13 Whoever scorns instruction will pay for it, but whoever respects a command is rewarded.

Today I am thankful for:

_____
_____
_____
_____
_____
_____
_____
_____
_____
_____

People to pray for/ Prayer requests:

_____
_____
_____
_____
_____
_____
_____
_____
_____
_____

Challenges that I may face today:

_____
_____
_____
_____
_____
_____
_____
_____
_____
_____
_____

Reflections about my day:

_____
_____
_____
_____
_____
_____
_____
_____
_____
_____

> ## IT IS TIME THAT YOU MOVE FROM TEARS TO TESTIMONY, YOUR STORY HAS TO BE HEARD

Day 14

PROVERBS 14

Proverbs 14:25 A truthful witness saves lives, but a false witness is deceitful.

Today I am thankful for:

_____

_____

_____

_____

_____

_____

_____

_____

_____

_____

People to pray for/ Prayer requests:

_____

_____

_____

_____

_____

_____

_____

_____

_____

_____

Challenges that I may face today:

_____
_____
_____
_____
_____
_____
_____
_____
_____
_____

Reflections about my day:

_____
_____
_____
_____
_____
_____
_____
_____
_____
_____

> **I AM EXTREMELY PROUD OF YOU! YOU GOT THROUGH THAT THING**
>
> Elder Angie Taylor Reames

Day 15

PROVERBS 15

Proverbs 15:13 A happy heart makes the face cheerful, but heartache crushes the spirit.

Today I am thankful for:

_____

_____

_____

_____

_____

_____

_____

_____

_____

People to pray for/ Prayer requests:

_____

_____

_____

_____

_____

_____

_____

_____

_____

Challenges that I may face today:

_____
_____
_____
_____
_____
_____
_____
_____
_____
_____
_____

Reflections about my day:

_____
_____
_____
_____
_____
_____
_____
_____
_____
_____

"

TREAT YOURSELF TODAY, YOU DESERVE IT

Elder Angie Taylor Reames

"

Day 16

PROVERBS 16

Proverbs 16:3 Commit to the LORD whatever you do, and he will establish your plans.

Today I am thankful for:

_____

_____

_____

_____

_____

_____

_____

_____

_____

People to pray for/ Prayer requests:

_____

_____

_____

_____

_____

_____

_____

_____

_____

Challenges that I may face today:

_____
_____
_____
_____
_____
_____
_____
_____
_____
_____

Reflections about my day:

_____
_____
_____
_____
_____
_____
_____
_____
_____

> **YOU ARE APPRECIATED, JUST IN CASE YOU NEEDED TO BE REMINDED**
>
> Elder Angie Taylor Reames

Day 17

PROVERBS 17

Proverbs 17:22 A cheerful heart is good medicine, but a crushed spirit dries up the bones.

Today I am thankful for:

_____
_____
_____
_____
_____
_____
_____
_____
_____

People to pray for/ Prayer requests:

_____
_____
_____
_____
_____
_____
_____
_____
_____

Challenges that I may face today:

_____
_____
_____
_____
_____
_____
_____
_____
_____
_____

Reflections about my day:

_____
_____
_____
_____
_____
_____
_____
_____
_____
_____

"

BUILD SO THAT YOUR LEGACY WILL KNOW EXACTLY WHO YOU WERE

Elder Angie Taylor Reames

"

Day 18

PROVERBS 18

Proverbs 18:21 The tongue has the power of life and death, and those who love it will eat its fruit.

Today I am thankful for:

_____
_____
_____
_____
_____
_____
_____
_____
_____

People to pray for/ Prayer requests:

_____
_____
_____
_____
_____
_____
_____
_____
_____

Challenges that I may face today:

_____
_____
_____
_____
_____
_____
_____
_____
_____
_____

Reflections about my day:

_____
_____
_____
_____
_____
_____
_____
_____
_____

> **IF TODAY WAS YOUR LAST, WOULD YOU STRESS ABOUT THAT THING YOU ARE STRESSING ABOUT? LET IT GO!**
>
> Elder Angie Taylor Reames

Day 19

PROVERBS 19

Proverbs 19:20 Listen to advice and accept discipline, and at the end you will be counted among the wise.

Today I am thankful for:

_____
_____
_____
_____
_____
_____
_____
_____
_____
_____

People to pray for/ Prayer requests:

_____
_____
_____
_____
_____
_____
_____
_____
_____
_____

Challenges that I may face today:

_____
_____
_____
_____
_____
_____
_____
_____
_____
_____
_____

Reflections about my day:

_____
_____
_____
_____
_____
_____
_____
_____
_____
_____

> **YOU ARE DESIGNED AND DESTINED FOR GREATNESS, KEEP PUSHING**
>
> Elder Angie Taylor Reames

Day 20

PROVERBS 20

Proverbs 20:24 A person's steps are directed by the LORD. How then can anyone understand their own way?

Today I am thankful for:

_____
_____
_____
_____
_____
_____
_____
_____
_____
_____

People to pray for/ Prayer requests:

_____
_____
_____
_____
_____
_____
_____
_____
_____
_____

Challenges that I may face today:

_____
_____
_____
_____
_____
_____
_____
_____
_____
_____

Reflections about my day:

_____
_____
_____
_____
_____
_____
_____
_____
_____

> ## SMILING IS CONTAGIOUS, DON'T COVER, SPREAD IT
>
> Elder Angie Taylor Reames

Day 21

PROVERBS 21

Proverbs 21:2 A person may think their own ways are right, but the LORD weighs the heart.

Today I am thankful for:

_____

_____

_____

_____

_____

_____

_____

_____

_____

People to pray for/ Prayer requests:

_____

_____

_____

_____

_____

_____

_____

_____

_____

Challenges that I may face today:

_____

_____

_____

_____

_____

_____

_____

_____

_____

_____

Reflections about my day:

_____

_____

_____

_____

_____

_____

_____

_____

_____

> **WRITE YOUR GOALS DOWN, YOU ARE BEING MOLDED FOR MORE, IT'S BIG**
>
> Elder Angie Taylor Reames

Day 22

PROVERBS 22

Proverbs 22:9 The generous will themselves be blessed, for they share their food with the poor.

Today I am thankful for:

_____
_____
_____
_____
_____
_____
_____
_____
_____
_____

People to pray for/ Prayer requests:

_____
_____
_____
_____
_____
_____
_____
_____
_____
_____

Challenges that I may face today:

_____

_____

_____

_____

_____

_____

_____

_____

_____

_____

Reflections about my day:

_____

_____

_____

_____

_____

_____

_____

_____

_____

"

STOP TRYING AND JUST DO IT, WE ARE DOERS OF GOD'S WORD

Elder Angie Taylor Reames

"

Day 23

PROVERBS 23

Proverbs 23:12 Apply your heart to instruction and your ears to words of knowledge.

Today I am thankful for:

_____

_____

_____

_____

_____

_____

_____

_____

_____

People to pray for/ Prayer requests:

_____

_____

_____

_____

_____

_____

_____

_____

_____

Challenges that I may face today:

_____
_____
_____
_____
_____
_____
_____
_____
_____
_____

Reflections about my day:

_____
_____
_____
_____
_____
_____
_____
_____
_____

> ## DO YOU KNOW WHO YOU ARE? INVEST IN YOUR BROKENNESS AND GROW
>
> Elder Angie Taylor Reames

Day 24

PROVERBS 24

Proverbs 24:29 Do not say, "I'll do to them as they have done to me; I'll pay them back for what they did.

Today I am thankful for:

_____

_____

_____

_____

_____

_____

_____

_____

_____

_____

People to pray for/ Prayer requests:

_____

_____

_____

_____

_____

_____

_____

_____

_____

_____

Challenges that I may face today:

_____
_____
_____
_____
_____
_____
_____
_____
_____
_____
_____

Reflections about my day:

_____
_____
_____
_____
_____
_____
_____
_____
_____
_____

> INVEST IN YOURSELF TODAY, YOUR
> FUTURE IS DEPENDING ON IT.
> PRAY ABOUT IT

Elder Angie Taylor Reames

Day 25

PROVERBS 25

Proverbs 25:21-22 If your enemy is hungry, give him food to eat; if he is thirsty, give him water to drink. In doing this, you will heap burning coals on his head, and the LORD will reward you.

Today I am thankful for:

_____
_____
_____
_____
_____
_____
_____
_____
_____
_____

People to pray for/ Prayer requests:

_____
_____
_____
_____
_____
_____
_____
_____
_____
_____

Challenges that I may face today:

_____
_____
_____
_____
_____
_____
_____
_____
_____
_____
_____

Reflections about my day:

_____
_____
_____
_____
_____
_____
_____
_____
_____
_____

> **YOUR FUTURE IS WAITING ON YOU TO ARRIVE- LEAVE THE TOXIC BAGGAGE**
>
> Elder Angie Taylor Reames

Day 26

PROVERBS 26

Proverbs 26:27 Whoever digs a pit will fall into it; If someone rolls a stone, it will roll back on them.

Today I am thankful for:

_____

_____

_____

_____

_____

_____

_____

_____

_____

People to pray for/ Prayer requests:

_____

_____

_____

_____

_____

_____

_____

_____

_____

_____

Challenges that I may face today:

_____

_____

_____

_____

_____

_____

_____

_____

_____

_____

_____

Reflections about my day:

_____

_____

_____

_____

_____

_____

_____

_____

_____

_____

" THANK YOU, JUST IN CASE NO ONE TOLD
YOU TODAY. YOU MATTER!

Elder Angie Taylor Reames

"

Day 27

PROVERBS 27

Proverbs 27:2 Let someone else praise you, and not your own mouth; an outsider, and not your own lips.

Today I am thankful for:

_____
_____
_____
_____
_____
_____
_____
_____
_____

People to pray for/ Prayer requests:

_____
_____
_____
_____
_____
_____
_____
_____
_____

Challenges that I may face today:

_____
_____
_____
_____
_____
_____
_____
_____
_____
_____

Reflections about my day:

_____
_____
_____
_____
_____
_____
_____
_____
_____

"

**SOMEONE IS STANDING IN THE NEED OF
YOUR PRAYERS, TAKE TIME TO PRAY
FOR OTHERS**

Elder Angie Taylor Reames

"

Day 28

PROVERBS 28

Proverbs 28:5 Evildoers do not understand what is right, but those who seek the LORD understand it fully.

Today I am thankful for:

_____
_____
_____
_____
_____
_____
_____
_____
_____

People to pray for/ Prayer requests:

_____
_____
_____
_____
_____
_____
_____
_____
_____

Challenges that I may face today:

_____
_____
_____
_____
_____
_____
_____
_____
_____
_____
_____

Reflections about my day:

_____
_____
_____
_____
_____
_____
_____
_____
_____
_____

Challenges that Linger for Today

> ## YOU WILL HAVE PEACE, ENDURE
>
> Elder Angie Taylor Reames

Day 29

PROVERBS 29

Proverbs 29:22 An angry person stirs up conflict, and a hot-tempered person commits many sins.

Today I am thankful for:

_____
_____
_____
_____
_____
_____
_____
_____
_____

People to pray for/ Prayer requests:

_____
_____
_____
_____
_____
_____
_____
_____
_____

Challenges that I may face today:

_____
_____
_____
_____
_____
_____
_____
_____
_____
_____
_____

Reflections about my day:

_____
_____
_____
_____
_____
_____
_____
_____
_____

LOVE LOOKS PHENOMENAL ON YOU

Elder Angie Taylor Reames

Day 30

PROVERBS 30

Proverbs 30:5 "Every word of God is flawless; he is a shield to those who take refuge in him.

Today I am thankful for:

_____
_____
_____
_____
_____
_____
_____
_____
_____

People to pray for/ Prayer requests:

_____
_____
_____
_____
_____
_____
_____
_____
_____
_____

Challenges that I may face today:

_____
_____
_____
_____
_____
_____
_____
_____
_____
_____
_____

Reflections about my day:

_____
_____
_____
_____
_____
_____
_____
_____
_____
_____

> **WHEN YOU WANT TO GIVE UP, GOD WILL ALWAYS GIVE YOU STRENGTH, CALL HIM**
>
> Elder Angie Taylor Reames

Day 31

PROVERBS 31

Proverbs 31:26 She speaks with wisdom, and faithful instruction is on her tongue.

Today I am thankful for:

_____

_____

_____

_____

_____

_____

_____

_____

_____

_____

People to pray for/ Prayer requests:

_____

_____

_____

_____

_____

_____

_____

_____

_____

_____

Challenges that I may face today:

_____
_____
_____
_____
_____
_____
_____
_____
_____
_____
_____

Reflections about my day:

_____
_____
_____
_____
_____
_____
_____
_____
_____
_____
_____

> **REPEAT: I MATTER, I MATTER, I MATTER. I AM LOVED, APPRECIATED, AND SUCCESSFUL**
>
> Elder Angie Taylor Reames

Congratulations!! You did it! You took the initiative to invest 31 days of your life to prayer. That is phenomenal. What plans should you take next?

Keep praying, keep trusting God. Continue to recap your day and learn how you can get the best out of each day. You can also use the next few pages to identify ways that you can become better or the things that have occurred that can be used for tools and building blocks for you.

Trust me, this is just the beginning of your journey. How do I know? Because I believe in you. The next few pages will allow you to reflect on your last 31 days. It is not necessary for you to complete all pages at once, please pace yourself, you are destined for greatness. Continue to pray and hear the voice of the Lord.

How have you grown in the past 31 days?

_____

_____

_____

_____

_____

_____

_____

_____

Were there any scriptures that ministered to your personal life?

_____

_____

_____

_____

_____

_____

_____

How have the previous 31 days positively impacted your life?

_____

_____

_____

_____

_____

_____

_____

_____

What areas do you think you still need to work on as it relates to your prayer life?

_____

_____

_____

_____

_____

_____

_____

_____

What goals will you set for the next 31 days?

_____

_____

_____

_____

_____

_____

_____

_____

How will these goals help you in your future growth?

_____

_____

_____

_____

_____

_____

_____

In so many ways, we gain clarity for what we need or desire and then find ourselves distracted by unnecessary things. We allow toxic people and situations to interfere with our spiritual growth, emotional peace, and mental health. One thing that I have learned is through constant prayer, God will put me back on track when I derail. Also, He will give me the confidence I need in order to maintain a constant prayer life.

You don't have to be perfect to pray. Your prayer life is often a reflection of your relationship with God. It is a form of communication. How often do you communicate with God? Is it only when you have a need or a want? I hope these past 31 days have helped you to change your perspective and enhanced your relationship with God. Perhaps you found yourself praying when you didn't have the book. You have prayed for individuals that you would have overlooked before- thank God for grace.

Starting today:

 ✦ Write a daily affirmation. It is time that you begin
    to speak over your life. If you have been doing it,
    be consistent. You will have what you say you will
    have. Ex: Today is already blessed, I am created
    with a purpose, I am successful, I am not

depressed, happiness belongs to me, I am fearfully and wonderfully made. My body is healed and my finances are blessed.

* Write/Reflect on your goals for the next 31 days.

* Forgive the person that hurt you. It is time, you have been holding onto the pain and it is interfering with your growth. Pray for them. Life is too short to hate.

* Love on Purpose

* Purchase a notebook if you don't have one, and begin writing your vision for the next year. If you already have one, great, add a year onto that one.

Proverbs is filled with wisdom; this is your time to pray and seek wisdom. Wisdom is experience, knowledge, and good judgement, it is the quality of being wise. Wisdom is knowing what is right, it is knowing what is true. Knowing what is right, incudes thanking God for what He has done, is doing, or what you need Him to do. This is your time to thank God for the many things that He has done. Or perhaps you want to thank others. So, what happens next? I am glad you asked. The next ten days, you will have the opportunity to say "thank you". Psalm 106:1 says, "Praise the Lord! Oh, give thanks to the Lord, for he is good, for his steadfast love endures forever!" For the next ten days, complete the letters of thanks that are found in the upcoming pages.

THANK YOU!

DATE: _____

Dear God,

I love you and adore you because/for

_____
_____
_____
_____
_____
_____
_____
_____

I confess that

_____
_____
_____
_____
_____
_____
_____
_____

THANK YOU FOR

_____
_____
_____
_____
_____
_____
_____
_____

Today I need

_____
_____
_____
_____
_____
_____
_____
_____

Scripture _____

DATE: _____

Dear God,

I love you and adore you because/for

_____
_____
_____
_____
_____
_____
_____
_____

I confess that

_____
_____
_____
_____
_____
_____
_____
_____

THANK YOU FOR

_____
_____
_____
_____
_____
_____
_____
_____

Today I need

_____
_____
_____
_____
_____
_____
_____
_____

Scripture _____

DATE: _____

Dear God,

I love you and adore you because/for

_____
_____
_____
_____
_____
_____
_____
_____

I confess that

_____
_____
_____
_____
_____
_____
_____

THANK YOU FOR

_____
_____
_____
_____
_____
_____
_____
_____

Today I need

_____
_____
_____
_____
_____
_____
_____
_____

Scripture _____

DATE: _____

Dear God,

I love you and adore you because/for

_____
_____
_____
_____
_____
_____
_____
_____

I confess that

_____
_____
_____
_____
_____
_____
_____
_____

THANK YOU FOR

_____
_____
_____
_____
_____
_____
_____
_____

Today I need

_____
_____
_____
_____
_____
_____
_____
_____

Scripture _____

DATE: _____

Dear God,

I love you and adore you because/for

_____
_____
_____
_____
_____
_____
_____
_____

I confess that

_____
_____
_____
_____
_____
_____
_____
_____

THANK YOU FOR

_____
_____
_____
_____
_____
_____
_____
_____

Today I need

_____
_____
_____
_____
_____
_____
_____
_____

Scripture _____

DATE: _____

Dear God,

I love you and adore you because/for

_____
_____
_____
_____
_____
_____
_____
_____

I confess that

_____
_____
_____
_____
_____
_____
_____
_____

THANK YOU FOR

_____
_____
_____
_____
_____
_____
_____
_____

Today I need

_____
_____
_____
_____
_____
_____
_____
_____

Scripture _____

DATE: _____

Dear God,

I love you and adore you because/for

_____
_____
_____
_____
_____
_____
_____
_____

I confess that

_____
_____
_____
_____
_____
_____
_____
_____

THANK YOU FOR

_____
_____
_____
_____
_____
_____
_____
_____

Today I need

_____
_____
_____
_____
_____
_____
_____
_____

Scripture _____

DATE: _____

Dear God,

I love you and adore you because/for

_____
_____
_____
_____
_____
_____
_____
_____

I confess that

_____
_____
_____
_____
_____
_____
_____
_____

THANK YOU FOR

_____
_____
_____
_____
_____
_____
_____
_____

Today I need

_____
_____
_____
_____
_____
_____
_____
_____

Scripture _____

DATE: _____

Dear God,

I love you and adore you because/for

_____
_____
_____
_____
_____
_____
_____
_____

I confess that

_____
_____
_____
_____
_____
_____
_____
_____

THANK YOU FOR

_____
_____
_____
_____
_____
_____
_____
_____

Today I need

_____
_____
_____
_____
_____
_____
_____
_____

Scripture _____

DATE: _____

Dear God,

I love you and adore you because/for

_____
_____
_____
_____
_____
_____
_____
_____

I confess that

_____
_____
_____
_____
_____
_____
_____
_____

THANK YOU FOR

_____
_____
_____
_____
_____
_____
_____
_____

Today I need

_____
_____
_____
_____
_____
_____
_____
_____

Scripture _____

I pray that this book has been a blessing to you. I encourage you to continue praying and studying. May God Bless you with overflow, increase, abundance, and miracles for the investment that you took in gaining a closer walk with Him.

Other publications from the author:

Perfect Imperfection: I am who I am

There is Purpose in your Pain

A 52 Week Prayer Journal- This is YOUR Year

You are able to purchase directly from the author at

www.angiereames.com

Books are also available at Books-A-Million, Amazon and
Barnes and Nobles.

ABOUT AUTHOR

Angie Taylor Reames, author of "Perfect Imperfection- I am who I am", "There is Purpose in Your Pain", and "A 52 Week Prayer Journal- This Is Your Year", is a native of South Carolina. Angie finds joy in encouraging others through prayer and positivity. Angie wants you to be encouraged in knowing that you have invested in becoming a better version of yourself and it is necessary. Angie is a Ordained Minister, Certified Life Coach, Founder of the Proverbs 31:26 Ministry, LLC, and a Woman of God after God's own heart. Angie aspires to inspire, encouraging others to be the best that they can be. She believes that there are occurrences when one must do a personal interview with themselves so that they can operate at the best of their natural and spiritual ability. Angie loves people. She enjoys family time, laughter, helping people, serving, and ministering to those that need to be loved, appreciated, and desire a sense of understanding.

Pure Thoughts Publishing, LLC